The Cat in the Hat's Learning Library

The Cat in the Hat's Learning Library

The Cat in the Hat's Learning Library

The Cat in the Hat's Learning Library

The Cat in the Hat's Learning Library

The Cat in the Hat's Learning Library

The Cat in the Hat's Learning Library

The Cat in the Hat's Learning Library

The Cat in the Hat's Learning Library

The Cat in the Hat's Learning Library

The Cat in the Hat's Learning Library

The Cat in the Hat's Learning Library

The Cat in the Hat's Learning Library

The Cat in the Hat's Learning Library

The Cat in the Hat's Learning Library

The Cat in the Hat's Learning Library

The Cat in the Hat's Learning Library

The Cat in the Hat's Learning Library

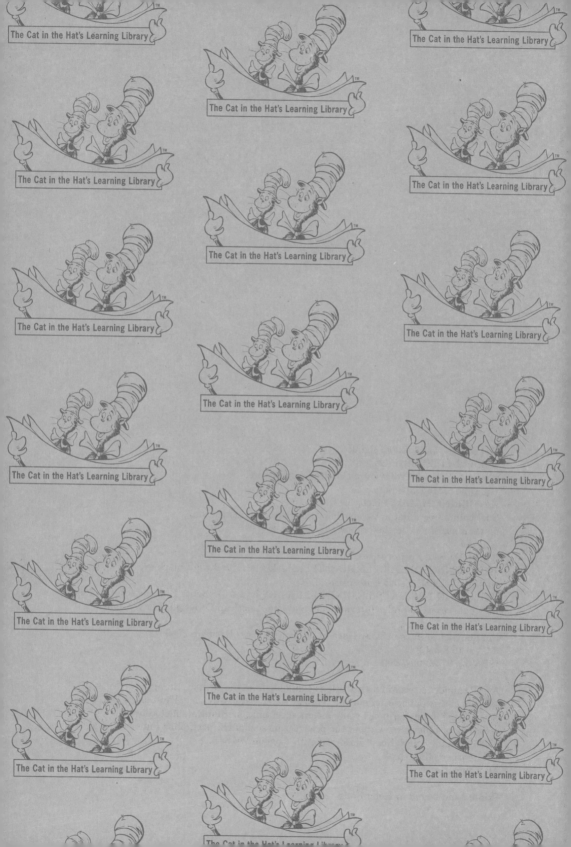

The editors would like to thank
BARBARA KIEFER, Ph.D.,
Charlotte S. Huck Professor of Children's Literature,
The Ohio State University, and
KATHERINE MADIN, Ph.D.,
Curriculum Coordinator, Woods Hole Oceanographic Institution,
for their assistance in the preparation of this book.

First published in the UK by HarperCollins Children's Books in 2009
3 5 7 9 10 8 6 4 2
ISBN-13: 978-0-00-728485-6

Printed and bound in Hong Kong

Clam-I-Am!

by Tish Rabe

illustrated by Aristides Ruiz and Joe Mathieu

The Cat in the Hat's Learning Library™

HarperCollins *Children's Books*

Hello! I'm the Fish.
To the beach let us go!
The Fish Channel asked me
to star in a show.

It is called *Fish and Friends*.
You can be in it, too.
Your mother will not
mind at all if you do.

Today on our show
we are off to explore
where the sea meets the sand
at the edge of the shore.

Here where the waves crash
in bubbles of foam,
you'll meet lots of creatures
who call the beach home.

Meet my friend Clam-I-Am!
She would like to say, "Hi."
She lives in the sand.
She's a little bit shy.

Clam-I-Am has two shells.
They have rings, you see here.
Rings show how much
she has grown every year.

See this hole in the sand?
Well, Thing One and I know
it means there's a clam
in the sand down below.

A clam has one foot that
helps it move about.
Clams pull salt water in
and spit salt water out!

Hello, horseshoe crab!
How did he get his name?
His shell and a horseshoe
are both shaped the same.

His shell shields his body
from any attack.
His eyes are in front.
His tail's at the back.

He has four eyes
but can't see very well.
To find food, he is helped
by his keen sense of smell.

2
1
4
3

They are not really crabs!
Every crab has an-TEN-nee.
Look closely, you'll see
horseshoe "crabs" don't have any!

Hermit crabs don't have shells,
so they look till they find
empty shells on the sand
that have been left behind.

Then they drag these new shells
everywhere that they go.
When the shells get too tight,
they need more room to grow.

So each crab starts to hunt
for a new shell to use.
There are lots to be found.
It is easy to choose!

My next guest is a sea star!
He told me today
that each of his five legs
is known as a ray.

If a sea star gets hurt
and it loses a ray,
a new ray begins
to grow back right away.

16

Sea stars are quite slow
when they move around.
Tiny cups on their feet
hold them on to the ground.

These creatures are molluscs.
Most have a hard shell.
Shells protect their soft bodies –
and do it quite well.

Seaweed doesn't have roots.
It grabs rocks, then holds tight.
Some seaweed grows up,
where it gets the sun's light.

Some seaweed you'll find
grows a lot deeper down.
Seaweed can be green,
purple, red, pink or brown.

When you pick seaweed up, you'll find creatures like these. They're sand hoppers, which are also known as sand fleas.

Seagulls fly near the ocean.
Their cries fill the air.
If you're eating your lunch,
they are hoping you'll share.

We learned this about seagulls.
Would you ever think it?
Seawater is salty,
but seagulls can drink it!

They're not fussy eaters.
They think it's a treat
if they find some dead fish
or some rubbish to eat.

Sandpipers run with
the waves at low tide.
They search with their bills
to find worms where they hide.

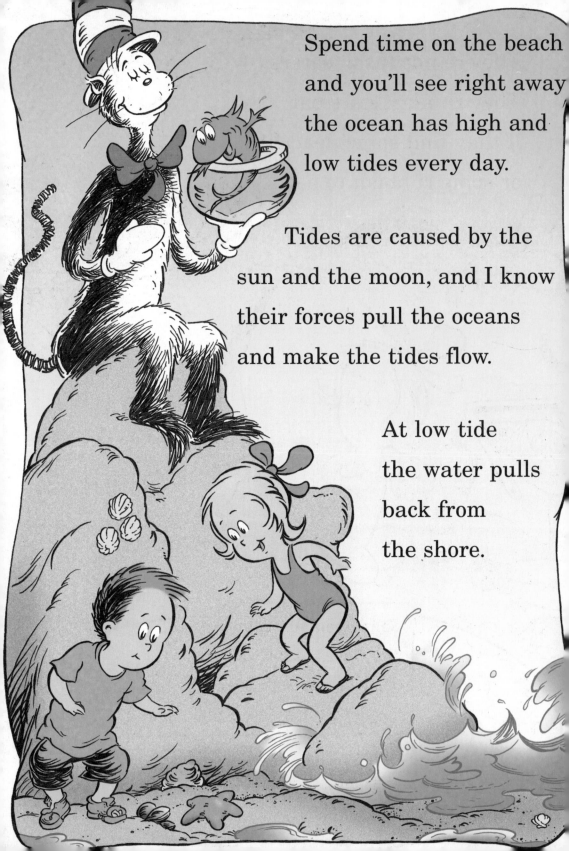

Spend time on the beach
and you'll see right away
the ocean has high and
low tides every day.

Tides are caused by the
sun and the moon, and I know
their forces pull the oceans
and make the tides flow.

At low tide
the water pulls
back from
the shore.

At high tide it is back
where it started before.

A tide table like this
makes it easy to see
when today's two low tides
and two high tides will be.

SEUSSVILLE
U.S.A.
AUG. 8

HIGH TIDE	12:47 AM	4.48 ft.
LOW TIDE	7:19 AM	0.58 ft.
HIGH TIDE	2:22 PM	4.36 ft.
LOW TIDE	7:50 PM	2.36 ft.

If you walk on the beach
at low tide, you will find
all kinds of sea creatures
the tide left behind.

See these clear blobs of jelly?
Thing Two and I fear them.
Some jellyfish sting!
So we do not go near them!

Some shells travel miles
and miles without breaking.
Find a shell in one piece and
you know it's worth taking!

Find a big shell like this.
Put it up to your ear.
You might be surprised
by the sounds that you hear!

This tidal pool
you will find is a home
to creatures who stay here
and who never roam.

These shells are called barnacles.
Watch them right here.

When a wave washes over them, threads will appear.

These threads are the barnacle's feathery feet. They grab food floating by for this creature to eat.

Not far from the shore,
sand is blown into dunes.
Dunes are home to crabs, birds,
rabbits, mice and raccoons.

When we go to the beach,
we make sure that we take
some old trainers,
a pail,
a small net
and a rake.

We wear our old trainers
without any socks
so our feet won't get cut
by glass, shells or rocks.

A net lets us scoop things
out of the sea.
A rake helps us dig
in the sand easily.

We put what we find
in our pail and then, when
it is time to go home,
set them free once again!

The next part of my show
I call "Go Ask the Fish".
I will answer three questions.
Pick one, if you wish.

why is the ocean blue?

GO ASK THE FISH

Ocean water is clear,
it just LOOKS blue. Here's why –

like a mirror, it shines back
the blue from the sky.

If you look at the ocean
on a dark, cloudy day,
it shines back the clouds,
so the water looks grey.

Why is seawater salty?

RAIN

LAKE

RIVER

Raindrops fall from the sky
and fill rivers, which flow,
washing salt off rocks
wherever they go.

Rivers flow to the ocean,
and as the years pass,

SUN

SOME WATER HEATS UP AND TURNS TO GAS

flows to...

OCEAN

some water heats up
and is turned into gas.

The salt in the water
is left, and that's why
oceans get saltier
as time passes by.

Wind blows over water,

and small waves then grow.

They get bigger and bigger

the stronger winds blow.

They keep going and growing
and head for the land.
Then the waves hit the beach,
and they crash on the sand.

When the strong winds die down,
then the waves die down, too.
Until the next time when
the wind blows on through.

Next, it's "Shop with the Fish"!
We have gifts from the sea!
You can order today,
and the gifts are all free!

We have pieces of sea glass.
The sun makes them glow!
They are pieces of bottles
that broke long ago.

MESSAGE
IN A
BOTTLE

SEA
SHELLS

They were tossed by the waves.
Over time, they were ground
by the salt and the sand
till the edges were round.

I've got lots of sea glass
and most of it's green.
This piece is the prettiest
I've ever seen.

We have beautiful driftwood,
and here's the best part –
it's ready-made sculpture,
real pieces of art!

Tossed by the wind
and the waves every day,
it was bleached by the sun
till it turned a light grey.

Oh dear, our show's over.
We must hit the road.
Please join us next time
for a new episode.

Come back to the beach.
You will smell the salt air,
hear the cry of the gull,
feel the wind in your hair.

You will find a seashell
to hold in your hand,
build a high castle,
dig your toes in the sand.

Everywhere that you look
you'll find creatures galore.
When you look even closer,
you'll find . . .

even more!

GLOSSARY

Antennae: A pair of long feelers used to sense touch and smells.

Barnacle: A tiny animal with a hard shell that attaches itself to rocks and other objects.

Bleached: Removed of colour; lightened; whitened.

Jellyfish: A sea animal with a body that is soft like jelly, is shaped like an umbrella, and has tentacles to sting its prey.

Keen: Sharp in sensing.

Mollusc: An animal with a soft body and no backbone.

Sand flea: A small hopping animal related to shrimps that lives in dry seaweed on the beach.

Sculpture: A moulded or carved work of art.

Shield: To defend or protect.

Tentacles: Long, thin body parts used to feel, grasp or sting.

FOR FURTHER READING

Oceans Alive by Angie Belcher. This stunning non-fiction book presents the underwater world and why we must protect this special place. There are simple descriptions of food chains, bizarre ways in which deep creatures support each other and ecosystems. Threats to marine life as well as conservation efforts are described in detail. Ages 4+ (978-0-00-723092-1)

A Fish Out of Water by Helen Palmer. A simple tale for young children. Ignoring the pet shop owner's advice, a little boy feeds his goldfish too much. What follows is an adventure that brings even the police and fire services out to help cope with a fish out of water! Ages 4+ (978-0-00-724257-3)

Wish for a Fish by Bonnie Worth plunges young readers from the sunny surface waters to the deepest ocean trenches in search of an amazing array of marine creatures. Ages 4+ (978-0-00-711108-4)

Josie Smith at the Seaside by Magdalen Nabb. Josie Smith is jealous of her best friend Eileen (who always gets whatever she wants). Eileen also gets into trouble all the time, but generally seems to come up smelling of roses! In this book Josie Smith goes to the seaside, meets a friend more horrible than Eileen and gets lost on the sands. Ages 5+ (978-0-00-674010-0)

INDEX

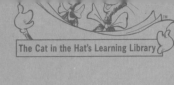

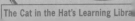

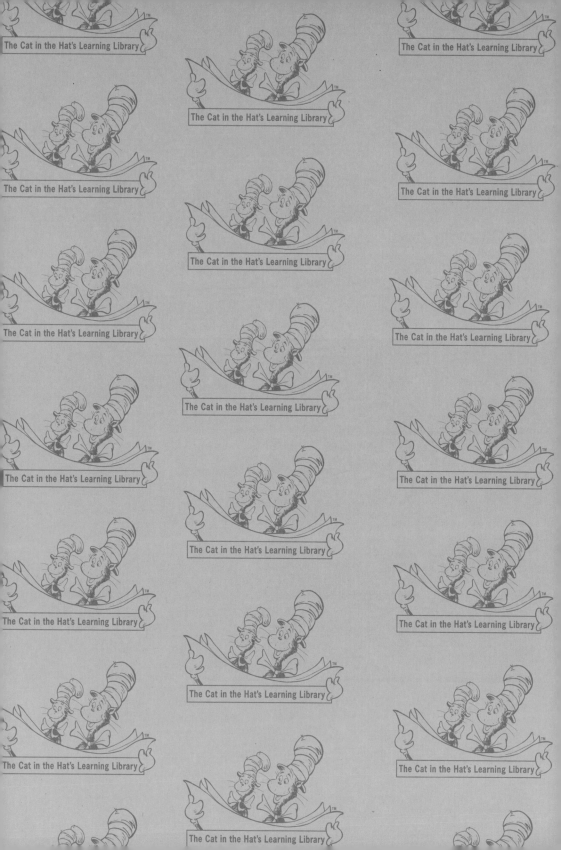